Youth on a Mission

The Future of Influencers

Richard R. Ramos

YOUTH ACTION GUIDE

Introduction

From the very beginning of writing my book, *From the Margins To The Mainstream, Preparing Latino Youth for Leadership in the 21st Century*, my desire has been to do my part in reaching out to, recruiting, and developing more youth mentors that in turn would develop more youth leaders.

The theme—*from the margins to the mainstream*—came to me as an idea, or internal message I received, several years ago. As I grew in my own personal journey of community leadership, I realized just how exceptional it was for a minority like myself to be in a position of mainstream influence. I consistently noticed that I was only one of a few minorities "at the table" providing solutions to community problems.

Because of these experiences it dawned on me how real discrimination is on a very practical level. I never really considered it before. But as I grew in my influence and opportunities in different communities to speak truth to power, the imbalance of that power became very obvious.

This realization became a burden. I remember sharing it with some friends as I began to develop it at that time as more of a topic to speak on and not a book to be written. However, the more I talked about it and thought about it, I decided it needed to be given more time and research to be developed into the full message and tool I envisioned for leadership development.

Once the book was finished, published, and shared with the public, I began to get feedback that a study guide was needed because other adults in leadership positions working with youth wanted to use it for a mentoring guide. Thus, I produced the current YOM Action Guide and you now have.

(You can purchase the full contents of the book, *From the Margins to The Mainstream*, on Amazon)

It gives me great joy to know that others are using this leadership guide to expand upon the stories, thoughts, and principles I share in the book to help more individuals experience greater levels of their true potential and inspire them to dream, run, fly, and lead!

Sincerely,

Richard R. Ramos
Santa Barbara, CA
October 2020

TABLE OF CONTENTS

Youth on a Mission Purpose, Principles, and Course Orientation..............................p. 3

YOM Topics

Session 1
What is Leadership?.. p.6

Session 2
Understanding Human "Being" ………………………………………………………p.9

Session 3
How to Discover Your Life Purpose, Vision, and Legacy…………………………….p. 15

Session 4
How to Discover and Develop Your Authenticity……………………………………..p. 21

Session 5
How to Develop Your Authenticity (Part 2) ……………………………………….….p. 30

Session 6
How to Overcome Negative Voices in Your Mind (Part 1) …………………………… p. 34

Session 7
How to Overcome Negative Voices in Your Mind (Part 2) …………………………….. p. 41

Session 8
How to Dream Your Way to the Top………………………………………………….…..p. 47

Session 9
The Power of Forgiveness……………………………………………………………..…..p. 53

Session 10
Destiny and the Power of One……………………………………………………………. p. 56

Youth On A Mission Orientation
Core Principles and Group Covenant

YOM Purpose & Group Commitment

Purpose statement:
To reproduce future *Influencers* to serve and improve community quality of life for all youth and families.

Getting to know group members:

1. Tell us a little about yourself: Where you grew up, your family, your hobbies, etc.
2. Why did you join "Youth on a Mission", and what do you hope to gain from it?
3. What are your thoughts about "Leadership"? What do you think it means to be a leader

The Seven Core YOM Principles

1. **The Psychology of Influence:**
   - The key to leadership is knowing how to _____ others.
2. **Understanding Human "Being":**
   - Learning how we _____.
3. **How to Discover Your Life Purpose, Vision and Legacy:**
   - Learning to write—or re-write—your own life _____.
4. **How to Develop Your Authenticity:**
   - Are you being the _____ you?
5. **How to Overcome Negative Voices in Your Mind:**
   - Improving your ability for _____ control.
6. **How to Dream Your Way to The Top:**
   - Imagination is more powerful than _____.
7. **Destiny and The Power of One:**
   - The power of one person's _____ to meet the community's needs.

Creating the YOM Group Experience

If we are going to have a meaningful experience in our time together, we need to talk about creating a safe place for everyone to openly share their heart.

Group Expectations:

1. _____
2. _____
3. _____
4. _____
5. _____
6. _____
7. _____
8. _____
9. _____
10. _____

Group Commitment:

As a Youth on a Mission, I commit to:

1. My own personal growth in emotional maturity.
2. Learn the skills to lead and influence others in a positive way.
3. Be true to myself in developing my life purpose, vision and legacy.

Name _____ Date _____

SESSION ONE

"People need to be reminded more often than they need to be instructed."
– Samuel Johnson

What is Leadership?

Purpose: To introduce the definition and psychology of influence and how we can use these principles for positive influence with those we are leading.

The subject of leadership is taught in many ways. But one of the best and simple definitions that sums up the essence of leadership was given by John Maxwell who says…

"Leadership is _____."

Psychology of Influence
In his book, *influence – the Psychology of Persuasion,* Author, Robert Cialdini talks about principles of how and why people are influenced, persuaded, and manipulated. *He calls them, 'weapons of influence.'* Below are four of those 'weapons':

1. _____: Giving something of value creates a feeling of obligation to give in return.
2. _____: people love to be popular and part of the crowd. This is why social media like Facebook and Tik Tok are so popular.
3. _____: people follow who they like.
4. _____: people tend to follow people who they believe are experts.

Discussion:
How can we use these *'weapons of influence'* and persuasion with integrity to benefit and not manipulate our followers?

1. The principle of Reciprocity:
- Give freely with no _____ in return.
- Give to meet a _____ need.

2. The principle of Social Proof (Copycats):
We are influenced most by the actions of crowds or groups of people around us. As a leader therefore:

- Don't always follow the _____.
- Be loyal to _____ – not popular fads, public opinion, peer pressure, or political parties.
- Avoid the _____ mentality: Following without thinking. Abandoning all reason, logic, and common sense.

3. The principle of Liking:
People are attracted to others who look like them, talk like them, dress like them, have similar background experiences, or have charismatic personalities.
Remember: _____ and _____ are not _____.

Another weapon of influence: _____.
This is not necessarily wrong, but what's important here for leaders is motive and integrity: *"Am I saying this to flatter, or do I really believe it?"*

Leadership with character adds value to others
- Be _____.
- Give honest _____—not fake flattery.

4. The principle of Authority
There is a difference between _____ authority and _____ authority.
- Appointed authority mainly _____ and _____ people that must follow him/her.
- Anointed authority is a gift that _____ the people you lead.

The purpose of power & authority is to provide:
- _____
- _____
- _____
- _____
- _____
- _____
- _____

Abuse of authority occurs when followers become automatically obedient without _____ for themselves.

SESSION TWO

"The essence of being human is being able to direct your own life." - Covey

Human Being

Purpose: To establish an understanding of the basic principles of how our "being" functions and methods for personal growth in maturity.

I. Keys to your success in life and leadership:
1. Discover the real you = _____
2. Develop the real you = _____
3. Find your path of purpose = _____ that sets you apart.

II. Understanding your "Being" – The real you
If we are to function in our full human potential, we should at least have a basic understanding of how our human "being" functions. Our "being" has incredible potential and the more we live in our potential and purpose the more it will benefit us and those we lead.

a.) Humans are three-part beings:
- _____
- _____
- _____

b.) Three basic functions of the body:
- _____ = my body needs _____.
- _____ = my body needs _____.
- _____ = I possess the capacity to produces other _____.

c.) Three basic functions of the human soul:
- _____ = I have the ability to think about my _____.
- _____ = my brain _____ before it thinks.
- _____ = I choose my actions. I choose how I think, feel, and what my attitude will be under all circumstances.

d.) Three basic functions of the human spirit:
- _____ = sometimes I _____ things before I _____ or _____ about them.
- _____ = this is where I connect with the _____ world.
- _____ = this is my automatic inner voice telling me _____ from _____.

Discussion:
- Which part of our being is most in control of our choices and actions?
- How can I know if my thoughts, feelings and choices are right or wrong?

The exciting thing about human beings is that we have the capacity to learn, grow, and change. We can improve our skill level in the things we want to do or become. We are not stuck at a certain level of intelligence or skill level. The goal of YOM is to assist you in discovering and developing all that you are, to grow all your talents, and live in your full personal potential as an individual and leader of others.

III. How to grow our "Being"

In the book, *Emotional Intelligence 2.0*, the authors describe "human being" development as emotional maturity in four parts:
1. _____: our ability to understand our emotions, what makes us tick, and how they affect our relationships.
2. _____: our ability to use our self-awareness to control our emotional reactions and choices.
3. _____: our ability to be in tune with others and understand where they are coming from.
4. _____: our ability to use our social—emotional awareness skills. These skills will help us to successfully influence, coach, inspire and lead teams of others to follow us.

Based on the above definitions honestly answer the following questions:

- Where is your self-awareness now on a scale of 1 – 10? _____
- Can you give an example—or share an experience that caused you to have better emotional self-awareness?

_____
_____
_____

- Where is your self-management now on a scale of 1 – 10? _____
- Can you give an example—or share an experience that caused you to better control your emotions and choices?

_____
_____
_____

- Where is your social-awareness now on a scale of 1 – 10? _____
- Can you give an example—or share an experience that caused you to better understand others?

_____
_____
_____

- Where is your relationship-management now on a scale of 1 – 10? _____

- Can you give an example—or share an experience that caused you to improve your influence and relationships with others?

_____
_____
_____

Key Point: Growing 'Old' Is Automatic – Growing 'Up' Is Not
One of the most important principles about leadership is learning how to "grow-up" in our maturity. In this next section we will examine the steps needed to grow ourselves into emotionally mature individuals and leaders.

A) Steps to Growth in Self-Awareness
Becoming self-aware is not something you arrive at but is a life-long journey.

1. Make time to _____, get _____, think, meditate, and/or pray.
2. Practice listening to your heart and _____.
3. Pay attention to your own thoughts and _____.
4. Think about your _____ about you.
5. Don't avoid _____ feelings.
6. Learn the things that push your _____.
7. Understand your _____ and your _____. What causes them?
8. Ask yourself why you _____ the negative things you do and say.
9. Check in with yourself after dealing with _____.
10. Get honest _____ about you from people who know you.

B) Steps to Growth in Self-Management
After you become more aware of your emotions you can then begin to manage them by using your reason to make wise choices.

1. Practice _____.
2. Freeze any decision making when _____.
3. Don't take yourself too _____.
4. Use your _____ to see yourself as an emotionally mature person.
5. Hang out with positive, _____ people as much as possible.
6. Be aware of _____ thoughts that lead to negative _____.

C) Steps to Growth in Social-Awareness
Good leaders are in tune with and connect with others where they're at in the moment.

1. Focus on learning people's _____.
2. Be aware of yours and others _____ language.
3. Be _____ in the moment.

4. Concentrate on the art of _____.
5. Develop a _____ about others and their values.
6. Imagine yourself in other people's _____ from other cultures.
7. Seek a higher—more understanding—view to get the _____ of the situation.

D) Steps to Growth in Relationship Management
This is where we put our emotional intelligence to use. As we grow in self-awareness, self-management, and social awareness we will become better leaders.

1. Be open and flexible in your _____.
2. Give others space, freedom and _____ to express their true _____.
3. Learn to agree to disagree, _____.
4. Learn to graciously _____ honest feedback.
5. Earn trust with _____ and _____.
6. Don't avoid confronting the complex or _____.
7. Acknowledge other's _____.
8. Show you care by _____ thoughtful _____.
9. Be humble, transparent, and _____.

Development by Assumption:
How would your behavior, actions, and/or usage of time change by the following:
1. Assume you only have two more years to reach your _____.
2. Assume others can always _____ what you _____ about them.

E) How to Find Your Voice
True or False?
"All humans have a deep desire to discover their uniqueness—purpose—voice in life."

Our Voice lies at the nexus of:
- _____
- _____
- _____
- _____

"When you engage in work that taps your talent and fuels your passion that rises out of a great need in the world that you feel drawn to by conscience to meet—therein lies your voice, calling; your soul's code." – S.R. Covey

Why is this—or is it—important?

- Finding 'your voice' is to experience life in your full _____.
- Your voice _____.

- When we find and express our unique voice, we _____ others to find their voice.
- You are never too old or too young to _____.
- The best way to predict our future is to _____ it.
- To create our future, we exercise our _____.

"If we have given away our present to the past, do we need to give away our future also…We can't allow yesterday to hold tomorrow hostage." – Covey

SESSION THREE

To be nobody—but—yourself—in a world which is doing its best, night and day, to make you everybody but yourself—means to fight the hardest battle which any human being can fight and never stop fighting. – e. e. cummings

How to Discover Your Life Purpose, Vision, and Legacy

First Things First

Purpose: The following exercises are to help you discover and define your Life Purpose, Life Vision, and Life Legacy.

Successful leaders understand three principles:

10. I am 100% _____ to determine how to develop who I want to be and what I want to do to live in my potential and purpose.
11. I was born on purpose for a _____ purpose.
12. I invest time and _____ in discovering and developing my specific gifts, skills, and talents to fulfill my life purpose.

Steps to Develop My Life Purpose:
Why am I here? What was I born to be and do? What am I living for?

Developing your purpose statement takes extended meditation and time alone. It requires getting in touch with your deeper, spiritual self that gives you a sense of 'meaning.' Here is an exercise to get you started:

- What matters most to me:
  _____
  _____
  _____

- What do I love to do? What activities excite me?
  _____
  _____
  _____

- List at least two special qualities about you (creative, athletic, artistic, intuitive, humorous, etc.):
  _____
  _____

- List how you usually express these qualities when around family, friends, colleagues, others (give one or two examples):
  _____
  _____
  _____

  Take one minute to answer the following two questions:
- 1) What would you do for a month with no demands on your time and unlimited funds?
  _____
  _____
  _____

- 2) List your top five values (family, success, wealth, fitness, integrity, faith).
  _____
  _____
  _____
  _____

Life Roles and Goals
What are my important roles in life (Husband/Wife, Mother/Father, Son/Daughter, student, team member, staff member, business owner, leader, aunt/uncle, etc.)? What are my important goals for each of my important roles? Write them below.

Role: _____
Goals:
_____

Role: _____
Goals:
_____

Role: _____
Goals:
_____

Role: _____
Goals: _____

Role: _____
Goals: _____

Role: _____
Goals: _____

Achieving your life purpose in your roles and goals also include your whole 'being.' Other questions to consider:
1. What are my mental goals for growth and improvement (more reading, study, podcasts, conferences, etc.)
   _____
2. What are my physical goals for growth and improvement (exercise, weight gain/loss, endurance, etc.)?
   _____
3. What are my spiritual goals for growth and improvement (prayer, meditation, scripture, etc.)?
   _____

Steps for Developing My Life Vision

Developing a vision for your life requires the use of your imagination, combined with your life purpose. Napoleon Hill described our life purpose as "a definite-chief aim." In other words, we must decide what we want to achieve in life. What we want to become, and how we want to express our purpose. He suggests that we write out a clear detailed description, a specific future vision. Author, Jack Canfield, in his book, *The Success Principles*, calls this process of purpose and vision, getting from *where you are to where you want to be.*

For our purposes in this course, I am going to give you three basic exercises for you to practice and use in developing your life vision.

1. **Take some time to get alone to think and answer this question:** Five years from now where would I like to be in my life both personally and professionally? Write out your vision and be as specific as possible: What do I see myself achieving? What has become my professional career? Am I married with children? Single? Have I bought property? Do I own a business? Am I working at my dream job?
2. **Spend time daily, weekly, or whatever feels right for you to meditate and visualize yourself in this five-year future.** See yourself owning your dream home. Driving your dream car. Owning your own business or working at your dream job. Happily married with (or without) children. See yourself taking that vacation, feel what it's like to have achieved your written goals personally and professionally.
3. **Create a 'Vison Board.'** A vision board can be created in several ways using poster paper, a cork board to put on your wall, or a notebook. The idea is to find pictures in magazines, or pictures you've taken with your camera or phone, that depict what you want to have in your life in fulfillment of your life purpose and vision. The city you want to live in, the vacation you want to take, the house you want to buy, the car you want to drive, the college or University you want to attend, etc.

The Five A's for Achieving My Life Purpose and Vision

1. _____: I am committed to be persistent in verbally affirming my ability to achieve my purpose, goals, and vision for my life.
2. _____: I acknowledge that I am responsible for the outcomes in my life. I acknowledge the power of my thought life and its role in my destiny. I will practice the habits of catching, changing, and replacing all negative thoughts that would hold me back from who and what I intend to become.
3. _____: I am committed to applying principles that are proven to be effective for achieving success and living in my full potential.

4. _____: I have written down a clear and specific purpose and vision statement that I will pursue with discipline until it comes to pass.
5. _____: I believe the right people, at the right time, the right place, and with the right spirit, will come into my life, for me to serve, and for them to serve me in pursuit of the highest good for all.

Steps for Developing My Life Legacy

As with developing the Life Purpose Statement, your legacy requires deep thought. Your legacy is about what you leave behind after your gone as an inspiration to others.

You want to consider who you are leaving your legacy with. Or who you were living your life work and story for? This includes family, friends, and colleagues. Our legacy is not just about our accomplishments. But also, about the people and community or communities we served.

Be specific and realistic about the legacy you want for you, your family, your career, and your community. The more specific detail you provide the easier for you to stay on track to create the specific story of your life as an inspiration to others.

For example: to say *"I want to be a good person to serve my community"* is vague. But *"to build a leadership program that reproduces parent and youth mentors to improve the health and safety of our community"* is specific.

As author Don Miller shares in his book, *Hero on a Mission,* your vision and legacy will probably embarrass you and scare you as you share it. But if you have a vision to make a meaningful impact in this world, 'you can't hide.' As Miriam Williams says, playing small in this world serves no one.

This idea of legacy may seem a bit out of your mindset at this point in your life. Nevertheless, the sooner you begin to think in these terms the sooner you will experience success and personal breakthroughs in your life.

Here are a few questions to get you started on writing your legacy:

- What do you want to be remembered for?
- What achievements are you most proud of?
- What do you want the people you studied with, played with, or worked with to say about you at your funeral?
- What were some obstacles you overcame before you achieved a goal you set for yourself?
- What are organizations, companies, projects did you make a difference in or successfully build?

- What were your most significant relationships?
- What word of advice, or message, do you want to leave your family, friends, and colleagues?

Begin with a few thoughts below. Use more paper as needed:

_____
_____
_____
_____
_____
_____

SESSION FOUR

The world is waiting to hear an authentic voice . . . not an echo of what others are doing and saying, but an authentic voice. - A.W. Tozer

How to Discover and Develop Your Authenticity
(Part 1)

Discovering Your Authenticity

Purpose: Your Life purpose, vision, and legacy is specific to you. You are not a 'copycat.' You are not trying to be someone you are not. You want to be true to yourself. That is what authenticity is all about.

This session begins with a story to illustrate where to look to discover ones unique, authentic value.

"Acres of Diamonds"
(Edited excerpt from the book, *University of Success*, by Og Mandino)

When going down the Tigris and Euphrates rivers many years ago with a party of English travelers, I found myself under the direction of an old Arab guide whom we hired up at Bagdad…He thought that it was not only his duty to guide us down those rivers, but also to entertain us with stories curious and weird, ancient, and modern, strange and familiar. Many of them I have forgotten, and I am glad I have, but there is one I shall never forget.

The old guide told me that there once lived an ancient Persian by the name of Ali Hafed. He said that Ali Hafed owned a very large farm, that he had orchards, grain- fields, and gardens; that he had money at interest, and was a wealthy and contented man.

One day the Old Persian farmer was visited by an ancient Buddhist priest, one of the wise men of the East. The old priest told Ali Hafed that if he had one diamond the size of his thumb he could purchase the county, and if he had a mine of diamonds, he could place his children upon thrones because of their great wealth.

Ali Hafed heard all about diamonds…he went to his bed that night a poor man. He had not lost anything, but he was poor because he was discontented. He said, ``I want a mine of diamonds," and he lay awake all night.

Early in the morning he sought out the priest…when he shook that old priest out of his dreams, Ali Hafed said to him: ``Will you tell me where I can find diamonds?"

``Diamonds! What do you want with diamonds?" ``Why, I wish to be immensely rich." ``Well, then, go along and find them. That is all you have to do; go and find them, and then you have them." ``But I don't know where to go." ``Well, if you will find a river that runs through white sands, between high mountains, in those white sands you will always find diamonds." ``I don't believe there is any such river." ``Oh yes, there are plenty of them. All you have to do is go and find them, and then you have them." Then said Ali Hafed, ``I will go."

So he sold his farm, collected his money, left his family in charge of a neighbor, and away he went in search of diamonds…at last when his money was all spent and he was in rags, wretchedness, and poverty, he stood on the shore…when a great tidal wave came rolling in…and the poor, afflicted, suffering, dying man could not resist the awful temptation to cast himself into that incoming tide, and he sank beneath its foaming crest, never to rise in this life again.

The man who purchased Ali Hafed's farm, one day led his camel into the garden to drink, and as that camel put its nose into the shallow water of that garden brook, he noticed a curious flash of light from the white sands of the stream. He pulled out a black stone having an eye of light reflecting all the hues of the rainbow. He took the pebble into the house and put it on the mantel…and forgot all about it.

A few days later this same old priest came in to visit Ali Hafed's successor, and the moment he opened that drawing-room door he saw that flash of light on the mantel, and he rushed up to it, and shouted: ``Here is a diamond! Has Ali Hafed returned?''
``Oh no, Ali Hafed has not returned, and that is not a diamond. That is nothing but a stone we found right out here in our own garden.'' ``But,'' said the priest, ``I tell you I know a diamond when I see it. I know positively that is a diamond.''

Then together they rushed out into that old garden and stirred up the white sands with their fingers, and lo! There came up other more beautiful and valuable gems than the first.

When that old Arab guide told me the second chapter of his story…he said to me, ``Had Ali Hafed remained at home and dug in his own cellar, or underneath his own wheat- fields, or in his own garden, instead of wretchedness, starvation, and death by suicide in a strange land, he would have had `acres of diamonds.'

Discussion: What is the moral of the story?

Lessons from Acres of Diamonds:
- We can miss "the diamonds" that we already _____ right in our own backyard = our own _____.
- We tend to look everywhere else for true _____ when it has been with us and _____ all the time.
- True wealth is first found _____.
- Like the man in the story - many people are unaware of the value they already have. They go through many years of searching with the wrong _____ in the wrong _____, looking for the wrong _____.

Key Point: Everything you need to be successful is not "out there" somewhere. Your true treasure lies in you and simply needs to be discovered by you.

The Diamond of Authenticity
- Your own _____- is your field of "diamonds."

- Authenticity simply means to be _____. To be true to your own spirit, true to yourself.
- Authenticity is your unique quality that sets you apart and causes you to _____ from the rest of the crowd.
- You are "_____" There is no one else like you. Embrace and value that about yourself.
- Authenticity is your core being or essence—your own special _____ of being you. It just comes naturally and is why others are attracted to you.
- The secret to taking advantage of your authenticity is _____.
- Authentic leaders are those who _____ and _____ the talent they already possess.
- Identity theft is not possible. No one can steal your _____.

Questions for Reflection & Discussion

- How real are we being in our _____ lives?
- Are we just acting out a pretend _____ of someone we want to be?
- Are we simply playing to the _____ and acting for the camera; Facebook, Instagram, Snap chat, Tik Tok, etc. caught up in a personality and lifestyle that's not real?
- Are we merely _____ on a string, speaking someone else's words, thinking someone else's thoughts, and living in someone else's personality?

Consider:
A lot of talent has been wasted and gone undiscovered simply because many youths were conditioned to look for images to copy rather than looking within their own hearts and minds for the authentic character and passion that they were born with.

Maybe it's time to re-write your life _____.

How to Discover Your Authenticity for Community Influence
The secret of success that all great people follow is that once they discover who they really are—and where their natural talent lies—they dedicate themselves to it, allowing no distractions or discouragements to get them off track.

The following principles will get you started on your own personal authentic treasure hunt:

1. **Pay attention to your _____**—Passion is found in those things that naturally excite, inspire, and motivate you. It is that certain thing (or things) that just clicks with you. When your passion is combined with your talent, it becomes an

unstoppable force that can achieve great things. It unleashes a potential that is only limited by what you believe you can achieve.

2. **Listen to the "_____"**— The community cry, is the main thing in your community in which the people show the greatest concern. It's the main problem affecting their quality of life. It's the issue that seems to get the most complaints from most of the people you are around every day. Thus, one aspect of your leadership can begin if you discover that the community cry is in line with your talent and passion, and you begin to feel the urge to get involved and be part of the solution.

3. **Listen to your "_____"**— Thoughts—ideas—in our head are one thing; however, the true passion and inspiration—the voice in our heart is another. How can you tell the difference between the "good ideas" in your head from the passion of your heart? The voice in your head will go away in time and switch to another topic. The passion in your heart will not go away, no matter where you are or what you are doing. It will become a burden that you can't seem to shake, and it will draw you back to the issue, time and again, until you begin to act on it.

How to Develop Your Authenticity
Purpose: *Discovering* your authenticity—your uniqueness—is only half of the formula to reaching your full potential. The other half is the *development* of what you've discovered.

In reading the story of those who have achieved great things, we usually find three aspects of their development:

1. _____
2. _____
3. _____

1. Self-Mastery and Choice
Self-mastery is a lifelong process and involves various disciplines and practices. For our purposes here we're going to discuss just three aspects of self-mastery beginning with the power of choice.

- The mature leader understands they have the power to _____ their response when facing difficult circumstances.
- We are not like _____ that can only react instinctively to their environment. Animals don't have the ability to think about their thinking and then decide to change their minds.
- We, on the other hand, can think about our _____. We can choose what to think about, how to feel about, and choose what to do about the things that happen to us in our environment. Nobody can take this freedom of choice from us. Nobody can 'make us' do, decide, or feel anything.

Nelson Mandela: *"Part of being optimistic is keeping one's head pointed towards the sun, one's feet moving forward. There were many dark moments when my faith in humanity was sorely tested, but I would not and could not give myself up to despair. That way laid defeat and death."*

As the saying goes, it's not what happens to us in life that determines our life, it's how we choose to think and feel, and what we choose to do about what happens to us, that creates our life.

Remember:
- We are not victims of our circumstances. We are victims of our _____ in our circumstances.
- We are not the product of only nature and nurture but also of our _____.
- Robots automatically react—humans choose to _____.
- The gift of freedom to act sets us free from a) the _____ mentality, b) the culture of _____.

Key Point: Regardless of what's happened up to this point (good or bad) in your life, it is never too late to exercise your power to choose to change how you're handling the circumstances of your life.

The story of Robert "Babo" Castillo,
As a youth, Babo was a gang member growing up in northeast Los Angeles in the 1960's and 70's. While he was hanging with his homeboys from Lincoln Heights, California, he discovered something special about himself—his ability to throw a baseball. Babo was caught up in living in two worlds. On the one hand, he had made the commitment of loyalty common to all gang members. On the other hand, he had become a star high school athlete with offers to play baseball in college.

His story is not unique. A lot of great athletes find themselves in this situation with a choice to make. Some choose to make it out of the negative lifestyle, some don't. Fortunately, for Babo, he had the support of his parents and coaches, and he made the right choice.

After high school, Babo decided to play ball at Los Angeles Valley Junior College in Van Nuys, California. After only one year of college ball, he was voted the most valuable player of the league and was drafted by the professional major league baseball team, Kansas City Royals.

However, the Kansas City Royals drafted him as a third baseman, not as a pitcher. Babo was a great all-around player, but his primary, most natural position, was that of a pitcher, not a third baseman. Once he realized that the Kansas City Royals organization was not going to let him "be true to himself," he chose to opt out of his contract. He decided to join the professional Mexican Baseball League because they would let him prove he could pitch at the professional and major league level. The rest, as they say, is history. After a year in the Mexican league he signed with the Los Angeles Dodgers, played nine great years in the major leagues, and was a key member of their 1981 World Series championship team.

Robert "Babo" Castillo played for the Los Angeles Dodgers and Minnesota Twins from 1977-1985. He pitched one inning against the NY Yankees in the 1981 World Series. He sadly passed away due to cancer in 2014 at the age of 59.

Discussion: What lessons can we learn from Babo Castillo's Story?
- It took a lot of _____ to choose to let go of his gang homeboys to pursue his baseball career.
- It took _____ in himself to decide to let go of an American professional contract for a contract for less money in the Mexican league.
- He chose to take control of his future by following his _____.

These decisions are prime examples of the power of choice, deciding to be the real you, and removing whatever obstacles you might encounter on the journey to authentic personal growth and development.

Self-Reflection
Take a few minutes to reflect on the choices you've made in your life—life-changing choices. Which choices are you glad you made? Which choices do you regret (if any)? Which are you contemplating now?

List them here:
_____
_____
_____
_____
_____
_____

2. Self-Mastery and Conscience

We have a built-in compass to help guide us in life, called our conscience. Our conscience is:

- _____
- _____
- _____
- Its job is to tell us when we are _____ or _____.
- It's up to us to _____ to listen to our conscience and act or not.

    The question for you right now is: Who or what are you listening to in making choices for your life? Are you listening to your conscience?

Suggested Exercise:
Using the list of choices from the above exercise, find somewhere you won't be disturbed for a while and listen deeply to your heart about where you are in life and what you are doing. Simply let your conscience be your guide.

Ask yourself questions like: "Am I truly happy with myself? Is what I'm doing really bringing out the best in me? Does my life make others in my family happy? Are the relationships in my life helping me or hurting me? Is what I'm involved in really the best thing for me, my friends and the community?"

A big part of your personal growth and development as an authentic leader will be this practice of cultivating sensitivity to hearing the voice of your conscience and learning to follow its guidance.

3. Self-Mastery and Mind Control

"When the mind discovers that it's powers are inexhaustible and that its faculties and talents can be developed to the very highest degree imaginable, and to any degree beyond that, the fear of failure will entirely disappear." – C. Larson

Self-mastery is also a matter of developing our mind and controlling our thoughts.

Question for discussion: Is it possible for our mind to be conditioned and controlled?
- Part of self-mastery begins by working to understand and control our thought life, beginning with our _____ about _____.

Consider this quote:
Sow a _____. Reap an _____. Sow an action. Reap a _____. Sow a habit. Reap a _____. Sow a character. Reap your _____.

Everything begins with our thinking. Everything is first created by the thoughts in our mind. (If you would like to learn more on this subject, scores of books have been written on this subject that can easily be found in any library, bookstore, or on the Internet.)

Discussion examples: True or False?
- "Thoughts are things."
- "Whatever you can believe you can achieve."
- "A person's mental attitude acts as a magnet, attracting the things, objects, circumstances, environments, and people in harmony with that mental attitude."
- "You attract to you the things you expect, what you think most about, and to whatever you direct and focus your mental energy on."

Learning how to use our mind is a lifelong process, and you can never learn too much, but the key is to practice, practice, and practice what you know!

Mind Control is a "re-minding"
To become an effective Influencer, you must capture the attention of the mind starting with your own. There are three fundamental principles and practices you need to master in order control your thoughts. You must practice becoming:

  a. A thought _____.
  b. A thought _____.
  c. A thought _____.

"There are times when I was listening to myself when I should have been talking to myself." – R.R.Ramos

- Some thoughts are more _____ than others.
- The habits of a negative mind must be _____ with the habits of a positive mind.
- The secret to growth and change is to keep _____ the principles of catching, changing, and replacing. In due time, you will replace the old mind with the new one.

A Battle for Your Mind:
In addition to the above three principles, you must also monitor:
- Whom you _____ with.
- What you _____.
- What you _____ to.

Don't be naïve about the influence the opinions of others and the media has on your mind and decision making.

SESSION FIVE

"A person with a high degree of skill or knowledge of a certain subject; a credible authority who defines what to pay attention to, what things mean, how things might work, and how things might turn out; an informed person who gets highly paid for their insight." – The definition of an Expert, Brendon Burchard, Founder, The Experts Academy

How to Develop Your Authenticity
(Part 2)

Purpose: The second part of the session is to continue learning the next two principles for further development of authenticity.

1. Developing Expertise

In order for you to fit the above definition, you'll need time, experience, and a hunger for knowledge that only comes through much study.

On the issue of time and experience, bestselling author Malcolm Gladwell writes in his book *Outliers*:

> "The emerging picture . . . is that ten thousand hours of practice is required to achieve the level of mastery associated with being a world class expert in anything."

He goes on to explain that ten thousand hours of practice is equivalent to about ten years. Once you know your life's purpose, you can set yourself on course to work on those ten thousand hours of practice so that in ten years (give or take) you become the expert "who gets highly paid for their insight."

a.) Experts Never Stop _____ .
- **What does it really mean to study?**
- Webster's dictionary defines *study* as: "the act or process of applying the mind to acquire knowledge or understanding of a subject; to think about; to examine in detail."

b.) Being in _____ to Study
- Studying is more than just reading books and memorizing _____ to take a test.
- Most schools don't really teach you _____ to study, they just tell you _____ to study.
- The mind functions best when it is unhindered by your _____.

c.) Hindrances to Study:
- Emotional _____ in our life can dominate our mind.
- Subjects that have no _____ to our passions.
- The _____ belief that more study will not improve your intelligence or _____.

d.) Helps to Study:
- Improving our capacity to _____.
- Embracing a _____ mindset vs. a _____ mindset.
- Studying what you are _____ about enables increased _____.
- Increased concentration = increased _____ to acquire expertise.

Story Illustration:
Ms. Erin Gruwell, the main character in the movie, *Freedom Writers,* the true story about a young woman who began her career as a student teacher in 1994 at Wilson High School in Long Beach, California.

Her first assignment was to work with the worst students in the school. In her book, *The Freedom Writer's Diary,* the students described themselves:

"Whether it was official or not, we all knew that we had been written off. Low test scores, juvenile hall, alienation, and racial hostility helped us fit the labels the educational system placed on us: 'un-teachable,' 'below average,' and 'delinquents.'"

One day, as she was trying to reach and teach her students, she caught a student passing a note with a derogatory drawing of a black student. This caused her to disrupt the class and yell at the student. She told them that it was for stupid stereotypes like this that caused the *Holocaust.* When she said *Holocaust,* the room grew quiet and only one student knew what the *Holocaust* was. Without realizing it, she had found the key to reaching these hardcore kids and decided to adjust her curriculum to teach something they could relate to—discrimination, violence, and intolerance.

This great teacher shows us what can happen in our ability to study when our emotional life is given a place of _____ and _____.

Ms. Gruwell went beyond the norm of most teachers today and tapped into the soul of her students.

Key Points:
- Expertise requires knowledge and gaining knowledge requires a lot of _____.
- Don't make the mistake of thinking there are _____ to gaining expertise.
- The sooner you discover your life purpose – the sooner you can start on your _____ to become an expert.

2. Private Practice
We are all familiar with the old cliché, "practice makes perfect," or as others say it, "perfect practice makes perfect." It may be an old saying, but it still holds true.

If we want to achieve greatness, be a cut above, stand out from the crowd, and become an authentic expert in our field, it will require an extraordinary amount of effort and dedication to the discipline of practice.

To read about or listen to successful Experts tell their story is important for a couple of reasons.

- It causes us to be _____.
- It serves to reveal that expertise is not about _____ that needs no effort, but rather about expertise _____ through the long hours of practice and discipline.

Fans only see the public performance. What they don't see is the all the dedication great performers are committed to in private, away from the lights and cameras that makes for the great public performances.

Key Points:
- Your expertise can help serve the _____ of other people.
- Your preparation, experience, study, and knowledge will add _____ to your audience.
- Your preparation, experience and knowledge will give your audience a life transforming _____.
- Your expertise can move your audience to another level of _____ of life.
- If you want to be the best at your craft: While others are "_____" you must be "_____" to be a cut above the rest of the pack.
- Natural talent will get you into the _____, but it's dedicated and disciplined private practice that will _____ you there year after year.

UCLA Legendary Coach John Wooden:
"I believe ability can get you to the top, but it takes character to keep you there…It's so easy to…begin thinking you can just turn it on automatically, without proper preparation. It takes real character to keep working as hard or even harder once you're there. When you read about an athlete or team that wins over and, over and over, remind yourself, 'more than ability, they have character.'"

The bottom line is—nobody can be you, or do you, like you do you. You possess the gift. The talent. The treasure. You come to a place in your life where you realize you have an obligation to share your gift because it was never meant for only your enjoyment, but also for the benefit and edification of the lives of others. And that's why you must devote your life to self-mastery, expertise, and private practice.

SESSION SIX

"Research indicates that the average person—that means you—talks to himself or herself about 50,000 times a day. And most of that self-talk is about yourself, and according to the psychologist researchers, it's 80% negative." – Jack Canfield, Success Expert

How to Overcome Negative Voices in Your Mind
(Part 1)

Purpose: To discuss the common negative voices that can hold one down, keep one back, and prevent one from living in their full potential.

The Presence of Our Past
Everybody knows the old saying, "sticks and stones may break my bones, but words will never hurt me." But nothing could be further from the truth. The fact is words have a very powerful effect on our hearts and minds.

Those negative words we heard from someone or from somewhere, like a song on repeat, keep playing in our minds over and over and can keep us from realizing our full potential.

LAPD Sargent:
"…there are so many insecure children out there. The ones I'm talking about are the ones whose parents verbally abuse them. I remember when I was in elementary school my late father when off on me for receiving a failing grade on my report card. He said to my mother, 'is this kid stupid?' but he said it in Italian, "stupido." I have never forgotten my dad's words. In fact this caused me problems in school for many years. To some this may seem like no big deal, but to me it was a real big deal and has caused me much pain."

In this first section about negative voices, we're going to discuss three of these voices and how to overcome them.

1. The Voice of the Fear of Failure

One of the most common mental hurdles created by our negative voices is the fear of failure. The fear of failure says: "but what if I try and fail?" or "maybe I shouldn't try that," or "I probably won't win anyway," or "I don't think I can do that again."

- This voice of fear creates a deep-seated _____ of self.
- We can experience a great _____ of accomplishment, but this voice causes us to doubt and lose confidence in ourselves to keep on accomplishing as a _____ part of our life.
- This negative voice gives us _____ to talk ourselves out of _____. In other words, we have developed a fear of failure.

How to Overcome the Voice of Fear of Failure
Great leaders aren't great because they've had everything come easy to them. Rather, they're great because they have tried and failed. Tried again, and failed, and tried again, and failed again, and again. But they continue to get back up and face their failure head-on and do not quit until they overcome. So, what is their secret?

Here are four simple principles (We already learned three of them in a previous session—but repetition is the mother of all learning) if you practice these consistently, they will help you overcome the fear of failure:

1. Face fear of failure _____. Don't be afraid to call it what it is. That is the first step to defeating it. Acknowledge your fear to fail and then consider what that voice of fear may be robbing you of: a better grade, a better position, a better relationship, a better job or prosperous career.

Take a few moments to think about things you want to do but don't because you're afraid you might fail: Are you afraid of what others will say? What others will think? Of being embarrassed? Are you afraid of being made fun of? Write down your fears here:
_____
_____
_____

2. Practice thought _____ - This is accomplished by paying attention to your thinking about yourself, catching the negative thoughts of fear, etc. and being aware of how this fear is holding you back from trying new things.
3. Practice thought _____ - After you are aware of your negative thinking, take control and change your thought from a negative to a positive thought about yourself.
4. Practice thought _____ - You must say the positive thoughts out loud to yourself. Remember: words have power and hearing yourself say positive words to yourself on a consistent basis is exercising the power of words to change your thinking, which will change your life.

Practice example:
1. Read the negative thought below to yourself:
"Why are you going to waste your time trying when you know you're not going to make it?"
2. Replace the negative thought by saying out loud to yourself:
"I can do this, I am good at this, and I know I will succeed if I give it my best effort and not give up."

How did hearing yourself say these words out loud to yourself make you feel? Consider the quote below by author, Marianne Williamson, who says sometimes our fear is not about failure:

"Our deepest fear is not that we are inadequate. Our deepest fear is that we are powerful beyond measure. It is our light, not our darkness, that most frightens us. We ask ourselves, who am I to be brilliant, gorgeous, talented, and fabulous? Actually, who are you not to be? You are a child of God. Your playing small doesn't serve the world. There is nothing enlightened about shrinking so that other people won't feel insecure around you. We were born to make manifest the glory of God that is within us. It's not just in some of us; it's in everyone. And as we let our own light shine, we unconsciously give other people permission to do the same. As we are liberated from our own fear, our presence automatically liberates others."

2. The Voice of Pride

Pride can be a positive, or it can be a negative. Negative pride is what we're talking about here. The voice of negative pride says: "I know better", "I'm always right", I'm smarter", "Humility and apologizing shows weakness."

- Negative pride causes _____.
- Negative pride _____ your mind from clear thinking.
- Negative pride blinds us to the truth about _____—which is the kind of blindness leaders can't afford to have.

The truth is:
- Pride blocks our willingness to _____.
- It deafens our ability to hear needed _____.
- Pride keeps us from seeking wise _____.
- It stunts our personal and professional growth and _____ us from those who can help us.
- It causes us to become _____; it keeps us stuck on things that may have worked in the past but are not working today.
- Pride strives to win the argument more than winning the _____.
- Pride shouts to exercise its power rather than exercising the power of _____.
- Pride says, "knowledge is king" rather than seeking the wisdom of _____ the bigger picture.
- The voice of pride lives in the sound of silence where _____ lurks.
- Pride is what keeps us from _____ why everybody else has moved on to new and better things.

How to Overcome the Voice of Pride

1. <u>Courage to change</u>
- Pride keeps us from seeing ourselves as part of the _____. If we can't see what the problem is, we can't fix it.

Dealing with pride is kind of like having the courage to look in the mirror right after we get up in the morning—scary, ugly, and messy. But it all gets better once we work on ourselves for a while.

2. <u>Feedback</u>
- Great leaders surround themselves with peers and mentors who will offer objective feedback even when _____ to their ideas and opinions.
- Without proper and challenging feedback, we won't _____.

- Strong feedback that says, "You're better than that," is something we learn to appreciate and makes us better rather than _____.
- Even our _____ and toughest critics can help us accept the hard truth about our performance and motivate us to improve.

Leadership is always about making things better, and we need feedback to make sure we are not deceiving ourselves into making things worse by patting ourselves on the back while everyone around us is quietly talking behind it.

3. Brokenness

Usually, when we think about breaking something, we think it will ruin it; like a toy, a glass, or something mechanical like a clock. We sometimes receive packages in the mail that say, "Fragile, handle with care", meaning that the object inside the package can easily be broken if we aren't careful. But the kind of brokenness mentioned here is a good thing—This kind of "breaking" can actually make us better.

- Brokenness is a way of _____ for fulfilling our purpose.
- It's a process of hardship, and perhaps _____ that brings you to a different, and often, better place in life.
- Brokenness gives you a different _____—a different _____.
- It gives you a better _____ in relationship with others.
- Brokenness is a process that _____ the best within you. It unlocks the treasure of empathy, understanding, patience, kindness, and unconditional love so needed by so many struggling with the issues of life and in need of help, guidance, counsel, and trustworthy leadership.
- Brokenness helps us to be slower to _____ and to rather think and wisely _____ to negativity.
- It helps us to be slower to _____, slower to _____, slower to _____.

A proud person is not someone needed in times of hardship, pain, and frustration. Pride is judgmental, harsh, small minded and intolerant of failure. A proud person does not allow the hardships of life to make them better, but rather causes them to become bitter.

Remember—the caterpillar's cocoon and bird's eggshell only serve a temporary purpose. Both need to be broken—cracked open. In both cases, what emerges is life more beautiful and more developed to live in their full purpose.

3. The Voice of Jealousy

Jealously is a peculiar thing. It's something we don't like to admit. Nevertheless, most, if not all, of us experience jealousy at one time or another towards someone or something else. Jealousy is envious, possessive, hostile, intolerant, and sees others as a rival. Jealousy is not healthy and, simply put, is a sign of emotional immaturity expressed by the following:

- Jealousy tends to attack or _____ others.
- Jealousy results from personal _____.
- Jealousy is at the root of why many leaders see other leaders as their _____ rather than as a potential _____.

How to Overcome the Voice of Jealousy

Whenever we hear that voice of jealousy creep up in our mind, it's time to exercise "positive pride": remind ourselves about the things we've accomplished, the things we're good at, the things we can celebrate to reinforce our self-worth, security, and self-confidence.

1. Making positive "I am" statements

- I am _____ in this world.
- I am not here by _____.
- I am a _____ maker and what I do _____ in life.
- I am a _____ to others.
- I am here on _____, for a specific purpose that _____ in this world.

2. Believe in your uniqueness

- Nobody can be _____ like I can be me.
- Nobody can do what I do, _____.
- I believe I have a unique _____ to make in this world.
- No one is a _____ to me because my contribution is mine alone to make.

3. Celebrate your uniqueness

- Nothing builds _____ like discovering and developing your unique gifts and talents.
- You don't have to _____ your uniqueness, your self-worth, or value. It's given on your _____.
- Your unique _____ already exists in you.
- There's nothing to _____ for. You already _____ it.

4. Demonstrate your uniqueness

- Express your _____ talent.
- Become known for your own _____ of leadership.
- Show up and make your _____ on the community and world stage.

- Don't hold back, don't play small, and don't save your best for "_____."
- Today is your day and now is your time to demonstrate why you are here and why you make a difference that is one of a _____!

This type of thinking and mental exercise serves to free me from the voice of jealousy. It allows me to celebrate others and be genuinely happy for the successes of others who might be bigger, or faster, or better, than I am at different things.

I'm good at what I'm good at. They're good at what they're good at, end of story. Why compete and feel threatened when we can celebrate and feel secure? We can accomplish much more when we choose to admire the differences in others and appreciate each individual's uniqueness.

SESSION SEVEN

Oscar De La Hoya, one of the greatest boxing champions of our time, said, *"Of all the battles I have fought in my career, none has been as tough as my struggle to gain my father's approval."*

How to Overcome Negative Voices in Your Mind
(Part 2)

Purpose: Continue to learn how to overcome more negative voices in our mind.

4. The Voice of Social Anxiety, Shame, and Self-Consciousness

Most parents are unaware of the affect our generational history has on our life and the life of our children. Olympic gold medalist and famous world-champion boxer, Oscar De La Hoya, shares in his autobiography, *American Son, My Story*, his inner struggles he suffered even as he was accomplishing his dreams as a world class champion boxer.

> *"From the outside we looked like the typical Mexican-American family. We didn't have any more or any less than other households in our East L.A. neighborhood. On the inside, though, there was something lacking, something very essential in the nurturing of a child. Maybe that was typical, too, of our neighborhood. We never talked about anything. We never had conversations around the house. I remember saying just a few words to my mother at a time and that was it. My parents never sat my brother and me down and talked to us about the birds and the bees or any problems we might be having. They never offered to help us with homework. They simply said, "We're the parents and you listen to us and that's it." The thing I regret the most is not telling my mother I loved her. She knew I loved her, but we never had that kind of communication*
> *. . . I don't want to say our household was cold, but there really weren't any emotions in evidence…My parents didn't know how to express themselves, especially my father. It's only recently that he has told me he loves me and has given me big hugs. I finally feel he's proud of me."*

Over my career in working with individuals and families I have found Oscar's story to unfortunately be a very common experience. Our past life and upbringing have a powerful influence in our present quality of life. But even if our past life was a negative experience the good news is: Once we understand the presence of our past, we can decide to take control and break the cycle of past generations hindering our current relationships.

Understanding The Difference Between Guilt & Shame
In his book, *Bradshaw on the Family—A Revolutionary Way of Self-Discovery*, Dr. Bradshaw describes what he calls a soul sickness:
- A deep sense of _____.
- Shame can be caused by the lack of _____.
- A lack of affection causes a feeling of _____ by one or both parents (physically and/or emotionally).

Bradshaw explained guilt and shame and the importance of knowing the difference.
- Guilt is feeling bad about something we have _____. Guilt says, "I've made a mistake."
- Shame is feeling bad about who we _____ as a person. Shame says, "I am a mistake," and therein lies what is at the root of our inner struggle that develops into shame and self-consciousness.

As children we are often the victims of a barrage of belittling remarks like: "What's wrong with you?" or "Are you stupid?" "You make me sick," "Idiot," or "Dummy." Thus, we can develop anxiety, self-consciousness and what Bradshaw described as "___."

How to Overcome the Voice of Social Anxiety, Shame, and Self-Consciousness

1. Acknowledge the shame and soul sickness
Acknowledging my "soul sickness" is the first step towards my healing.
2. Use verbal affirmations:
    a) My actions might be a mistake. But I am not a _____.
    b) I am worthy of _____.
    c) I am good at _____.
    d) What I love about me is _____.

3. Take action and learn to function in the "zone"
As an athlete, we experience the difference between performing in the "zone or flow" and performing in "self-consciousness."

- My performance is best when I focus on the task and not the _____.
- My effectiveness is best when I concentrate on using my skills and not how _____ while using my skills.
- I can take action to get out of my _____ zone and into the _____ zone.

5. The Voice of Procrastination—"Mañana Mentality"

- When it comes to _____ there's no place for procrastination—or the *mañana* mentality.
- Leaders might have their days of laziness, cutting corners, putting things off, and avoiding challenges. The difference is that leaders don't allow it to become their _____—always putting off for tomorrow what can be done today.
- It's tempting to cave into the _____ pressure—not wanting to be unpopular, looking for the shortcut, taking the easy way out.

Key Point: If you want to be effective and credible as a leader, there's really no room for excuses about why we haven't followed through on our word.

How to Overcome the Voice of Procrastination:

1. Grow in emotional _____—No excuses or explanations. Rather than being offended, angry, and resentful with someone who has the courage to point out the truth about your laziness, lack of follow-through, and

mañana mentality, be thankful, admit your guilt, stop wasting time, and get on with the business of personal change and growth.
2. Determine what your _____ is in life—Decide what is important to you. Write down personal and professional goals. Ask and answer such questions as: Why are these goals important to me? Why would achieving these goals improve my life?
3. Make sure your "_____" is bigger that your "_____." In other words, you must know why you are doing what you are doing as a source of motivation especially during the tough times.
4. Don't be controlled by your _____—Emotionally mature leaders learn how to dig deep in their hearts and find that inner fire that allows us to overcome our moods and perform as needed regardless of circumstances.
5. Tell _____—Oftentimes the best way to achieve a desired goal is to write it down, write the date you will do it, and then go tell someone who will hold you accountable to do what you said you were going to do.

Practice Now: Below write down at least one goal you have and the date you think you can accomplish it.
_____

6. The Voice of Intimidation
"He didn't…so much as nod. And he damn sure didn't smile…he held your gaze for too long, and those blue eyes were chilling. I've learned with guys who look like that, guys who think they're bad asses, you don't keep your distance from them. You move in closer." – Edward Follis, The Dark Art, My undercover life in Global Narco-Terrorism.

Intimidation is an emotional imbalance of fear that causes you to shrink and be unable to act. We make it worse by letting our minds run wild with all kinds of negative ideas and "what if" scenarios that only serves to empower the threat even more. It's a common tactic of bullies who seek to take advantage of us because they have the upper hand in position and power (like a landlord, boss, manager, principal, or a policeman).

Some Examples of Intimidation:

1. When a person _____ you—We're usually not intimidated by the person who talks too much as we are of the person who says nothing when we try to engage them in a conversation.
2. _____—Sometimes just by a person's mere reputation as a celebrity or person of authority and social status, we can feel inferior and afraid to challenge or approach such an individual.
3. _____—We are often intimidated when we think that someone is smarter or knows more about a particular topic than we do.

4. _____—Muhammed Ali was probably best known for using this tactic to intimidate his opponents before a big fight. His crazy, obnoxious, loud, and unpredictable behavior was all a strategy to intimidate his opponent psychologically.
5. _____—Usually all that's needed to use the psychology of intimidation is the use of verbal threats.
6. Bold _____—It's like playing a game of poker where our opponent tries to bluff and intimidate by giving the perception, he has the upper hand. How many times is the bluff not called because of intimidation? Our opponent never had to show their hand because we were too intimidated to make the call.

How to Overcome the Voice of Intimidation

1. _____—We can't allow ourselves to be intimidated by thinking we're not smart enough, it's not our place, or that we have no voice. By showing up you will encourage others not to be intimidated either.
2. _____—It takes courage to finally speak up in personal or public places or meetings. However, your opinion—your voice—may make the difference in personal or community influence for the better.
3. _____—At times a leader must exercise self-control and not show emotion. Expressing your anger might feel good at the moment, but it will cost you respect and the confidence of others. Sometimes the best response in heated moments is silence. On the other hand, there are times when you're past sizing-up the situation and you know it's time to speak-up, and the wise and mature leader will know the difference.

Closing Thoughts on Leadership:

1.   Don't confuse leadership with _____ position. Leadership is not always about what we do in public, but it is always about who we are in private. That's where the victory comes, that's where these voices are defeated, and that's where the character of leadership is built.
2.   Don't underestimate _____ you are. Stop doubting your abilities. Stop letting your failures intimidate you. Failing does not make you a failure as long as you get back up and keep trying rather than being intimidated into ineffectiveness and silence.

A word of encouragement:
"Your message is too important. Your story needs to be heard. Your gifts need to be shared. Your expertise needs to be exposed to a wider audience. What are you waiting for? You don't need anyone other than yourself to give you permission to achieve excellence, take a risk, and be the best you can be. If you won't give yourself permission, then I will…*I hereby give you permission to go out and kick some butt in this world by manifesting your gifts and talents to serve others and make a difference while there's still time.* There you have it! Now get out there and get started today!" – R. R. Ramos

Practice Now: Below write down at least one emotion or negative voice you have battled with that you will now begin to overcome by using the principles taught here.

_____
_____
_____

SESSION EIGHT

To dream anything you want to dream—that is the beauty of the human mind. To do anything you want to do—that is the beauty of the human will. To trust yourself to test your limits—that is the courage to succeed. –Bernard Edmonds

How to Dream Your Way to the Top

Purpose: This session begins by sharing a great individual story that illustrates exactly why having a dream, or vision, is an important piece of the leadership journey.

Richard Montanez is his name, and this is his "Cookie" story...

From Cookies to The Corporate Jet
Ever since he was a child, Richard's creative mind was at work. He talks about how he started his first business in elementary school by selling the burritos his mom would make him for lunch. He says all the white kids would rather eat the burritos than the sandwiches they brought from home. This led him to more dreaming and imagining what he could do to have more than what others were telling him he could achieve.

Richard explains how in grammar school (that's what we called it back in the day) there used to be two lines after school: One for the white kids and another for the Mexican kids. The difference was the white kids' line went into a bungalow where they received cookies and milk for a snack; however, there weren't any cookies or milk in the other line, just homework to do before going home.

One day Richard was really, really, hungry, and wondered if he could get away with getting in the *white line* and not be noticed, "Hunger will cause you to dream big," as he likes to say. The other kids told him he was crazy, but somehow, he still hoped that the teachers wouldn't notice him even though his skin was dark brown, and he had jet-black hair. As he got closer and closer to the door, he began to sweat and get nervous, but his hunger was stronger than his nervousness. When he finally got to the front of the line the teacher looked at him and asked, "Richard, what do you think you're doing?" In his shaky, but hungry voice, he asked if he could go in and get some cookies. The teacher looked at him for a long moment. He could tell she was thinking about it and probably a little nervous that this little Mexican had put her on the spot in front of everyone. She then gave him a little grin of a smile and replied, "Yes you can!"

What a difference Richard made that day, not only for himself but also for the entire school and all the other Latino kids watching this *hungry dreamer.* But that's only the beginning of the story.

As he grew older, Richard got involved in the gang lifestyle. Like most boys who look up to their dads, he followed in his dad's footsteps as a bona-fide gangster. He tells how his father once took him along on a drive-by shooting when he was only twelve years old. Yet, aside from all the gangbanging, Richard's dad also taught him about hard work and would make him mow lawns with him every Saturday to earn money. Learning the value of hard work eventually paid off in a huge way.

As he got older, Richard went out on his own looking for a job. He ended up landing a job as a janitor for the corporation, Frito-Lay, the corporation that produces many different snacks and drinks.

Every day at the Frito-Lay plant, huge amounts of these products were leftover and thrown away. One day he noticed that his co-workers were taking the leftover Cheetos and putting salsa on them and eating them as snacks during break times.
Being the dreamer that he was, all of a sudden, he had a great idea. The more he thought about it, the more he became convinced it could work. He didn't know how it could be done, but he just somehow knew it could be. He had a vision. A dream.

Finally, he mustered up the courage to approach the CEO of the Corporation to ask if he could share the idea with him.

"Richard," his boss said, "What idea do you have that you want to meet with me?"

Richard replied, "I think I have an idea that could make a lot of money and I would like a chance to present it."

His boss gave him a funny look but agreed and gave him two weeks to prepare to make his presentation. Excited about the opportunity he went all out. He bought a suit and tie, which he had never done before. He bought a book on marketing and making presentations and read and studied the best he could.

"I had no idea what I was doing", he later admitted. All he had was an idea, a dream, and knew if he could get it across, it would be big.

The day finally came. He put on his new suit and drove to work for the first time like he was an executive. It sure felt better than coming to work in his dirty jeans and tennis shoes as a janitor. Before he went in the building, he took a little time to study his notes, and then, with sweaty, nervous hands, he walked into the building and over to the elevators he normally rode to move from floor to floor to clean. This time he went up to the executive floor of the corporate building, growing more and more anxious, hearing and counting each sound of the "ding" as the elevator passed each floor.

In the executive meeting room, all the executives were sitting around the table wondering and waiting to see what the little Mexican janitor could possibly be up to.

Richard had a swarm of butterflies madly flying around inside his stomach as he was given the chance to make his presentation. He couldn't help but notice the disgusted look on all their faces as they sat and listened to him struggle to explain himself. "I made a complete fool of myself," he said.

Then during the presentation, one of the vice presidents (whose job it was to come up with creative ideas) asked him, "Okay Richard, so how much of the market are we going to get if we do this idea of yours?" Richard said, "I don't know, I haven't read that chapter yet."

As they all sat there and looked at him with disdain, all of a sudden, a picture of the chip racks in the store came into his mind and he quickly added, "But, I think if we do this we will get at least this much of the market," stretching out his arms from side to side.

At that they all began to laugh at him, except the CEO and president of the corporation. He was not laughing but sat there thinking. He then stood up and said, "Gentlemen, this man has just given us an idea, that is going to make millions of dollars."

You see, Richard Montanez is the man credited with creating what you and I today know as "Hot Cheetos", which have become one of the biggest selling products for Frito-Lay, making them literally billions of dollars each year. This idea took Richard from the corporate janitor to one of the regional corporate vice presidents of Frito- Lay. All because he dared to dream!

Richard says, "The corporate jet is much better than the back of my father's truck."

Richard is a prime example of a Latino leader who applied his creative abilities to dream and moved from the margins to the mainstream of the corporate world. Today he shares his story every chance he gets (he also wrote a book about it and a movie is in the works to be directed by actress, Eva Longoria) to inspire young Latino leaders that you too can "make it" if you dare to dream.

Do you have a dream?
What is your dream? Do you still have it? Are you still pursuing it? Has it changed? What are you doing to achieve your dream? For some, you've definitely known for years exactly what you want to do for your professional career. For others, you're still not quite sure and that's okay, too. Don't worry. It'll come to you.

Albert Einstein said:

"It's more powerful to live in your imagination than to live in your memory. Imagination is more important than knowledge. For knowledge is limited to all we now know and understand while imagination embraces the entire world, and all there ever will be to know and understand."

By living in our imagination, we just need to do more purposeful daydreaming; more thinking and more imagining how things might look better, work better, and feel better.

How to Unleash Your Imagination

1. Get over what others will _____ about you – Fear of what others will think or say, fear of the unfamiliar, and fear of failure are the three most common obstacles that have to be overcome.
2. Expose your _____ – Don't limit your mind to the familiar. Expose your mind to the thoughts and work of other people of other times, places, ethnicities, and cultures. Force yourself to read widely and deeply. Stretch the muscles of your mind. If possible, travel to other cities, states, and countries. If you don't have the money for those things, drive or take the bus to different parts of your own city or town. There must be a lot of places where you live that you have never visited or even noticed. In other words, become a tourist in your own backyard (Remember the "Acres of Diamonds" story).
3. Change your _____ – Be aware of your habits and routines. Switch them up every so often. Take a different route to work or school. Break up your routines. Why is this important? Because when you follow the same routine every day, day after day, your brain more or less goes to sleep and overlooks things you would otherwise have noticed that might give you a better perspective, understanding, or idea that you need.
4. Invest in _____ – Find a way to be around people of vision that have accomplished big things. Invest in yourself and pay to read their books, listen to their audio programs, and attend their conferences and seminars.
5. Set aside time to _____ – Close your eyes and use your imagination. You will receive the big thoughts and ideas to guide you to your purpose in life. Dr. John Maxwell, one of today's premier global leaders, says in his book, *Thinking for a Change,* that he has a specific chair he sits in on specific days for a specific amount of time, just to think.
6. Trust your _____ – Have confidence in your God-given talent. Once you believe something can be done, you unleash your mind's abilities to find a way to make it happen for you. If you believe it or don't believe it, either way, your mind will go to work to prove yourself right. Take the positive road and believe as Walt Disney said, "If you can dream it, you can achieve it."
7. Don't put your mind on _____ – Nothing grows in ice. Put away all the things that cause your mind to freeze, such as fear, tradition, conventional

wisdom, over-analyzing, suspicion, fixed routines, and other limiting environments that block your mind from sprouting new ideas. Nature teaches us that new life does not grow in the snow.
8. Don't let _____ slip away – Write down your ideas. Record them on a voice recorder when they come into your mind. Talk about them to others. Never take for granted or minimize the inspiration you receive. Great ideas don't always come at the time you are thinking about the things that interest you.
9. Be a _____ catcher – After spending a lot of time reading, researching, studying, and thinking about something, the right idea or solution will come. When it comes, capture it by writing it down or recording it. Think of yourself as a butterfly catcher. The butterfly usually lands on a flower only for a moment, but then flies away to another flower. They are not very difficult to catch; however, they are not that easy to catch if you are not prepared to act quickly. Big thoughts and dreams are like that—they come and go quickly.

Key Point:
- When your imagination is combined with your talent and passion, it can create the kind of ideas that become a great movie, a great book, a new hit song, or message that generates a movement to provide solutions to complex problems to the benefit of your community, the country, or even the whole world.

"Focused thought and emotion create your reality." = Marc Allen

In our final session, we examine the lives of some of the greatest leaders in history to demonstrate destiny and the power of one person willing to use their imagination and act on their dreams to improve the lives of others. However, before moving on to that session, there is one more vital principle we must practice that is perhaps most important in the process of living in your full potential and dreaming your way to the top.

SESSION NINE

"I learned that forgiveness is the most powerful and absolute prerequisite mental shift necessary to empowering our potential . . . true forgiveness is about letting go of a way of life." - Dr. Eldon Taylor

"We must develop and maintain the capacity to forgive. He who is devoid of the power to forgive is devoid of the power to love. There is some good in the worst of us and some evil in the best of us. When we discover this, we are less prone to hate our enemies." – Dr. Martin Luther King Jr.

The Power of Forgiveness

Purpose: The freedom to live in the power of our full potential as human beings is to forgive. Therefore, part of living in our potential is identifying areas in our lives where forgiveness is needed.

Don't deceive yourself. It is impossible to be a human being and not be hurt along the way. What we decide to do with those hurts, however, is the key to whether the hurts make us a victim of them or a victor over them.

Think on These Things:
1. The ability to forgive is a decision of our _____.
2. Some _____ are harder to forgive than others. But to be free we must forgive.
3. Some _____ are harder to forgive than others. But to live fully we must forgive.
4. Like any other skill, forgiveness must be desired, learned, demonstrated, nurtured and continuously _____.
5. As the years go by if we don't communicate forgiveness our hearts begin to _____.
6. As time passes, suppressed issues become harder to forgive and revenge, anger, guilt, and/or shame take root in our hearts, and we are no longer in _____.
7. Choosing not to forgive keeps parts of you _____ away.
   - By not forgiving I _____ myself by ignoring my _____.
   - By ignoring my conscience, I _____ myself into thinking it's okay not to forgive.
   - When I don't forgive you, I need you to keep being angry and unforgiving of me to _____ that I'm _____ not to forgive you.
   - Our pride, anger, and wanting revenge prevents forgiving others because if I forgive, it means I have no one to _____ and must now take responsibility for my life.
8. Hanging on to bitterness and revenge develops _____ and _____ hearts unfit for good and positive leadership.

The power in the principle of forgiveness is experienced in three ways:

1) Being forgiven by someone you _____.
2) Forgiving _____ who have hurt you.
3) Forgiving _____ for past regrets.

Forgiveness takes me from victim to victor! Although this is not an easy thing to do, the results of reconciliation are worth the struggle to learn how to forgive even if the person is no longer in your life; it is still a very liberating life changing experience to forgive.

Remember: You don't need an _____ to forgive the person who hurt you.

The decision to forgive does not come as easy for some as for others. In cases like this:

- Consider seeking for the _____—the willingness—to let go of the anger and bitterness so you will be set free to be all you can be.
- Remember, forgiveness is _____, but trust must always be _____. Forgiving someone doesn't mean you have to trust them, too.
- If you choose to forgive someone who has violated your trust, you will be free from _____ towards him or her. But they are still in your _____ to earn your trust by proving their character over a reasonable amount of time.

Nelson Mandela Story of Forgiveness

In 1963, he was put into a prison cell to quiet his voice and end his threat to the government; however, his imprisonment only served to strengthen his voice of influence, as he became the most respected leader in South Africa while in prison.

Years of public pressure on the government became overwhelming, and he was finally released from prison in 1990. Four years later, in May of 1994, he became the first democratically elected black president of South Africa.

After learning about all the injustices this man went through, no one would fault him for being full of hatred and wanting revenge on his persecutors. Once he came into power as the president of the country, we could expect him to hunt down his persecutors and take his revenge; however, Nelson Mandela is not your normal leader. He chose the path of peace and forgiveness instead. After being elected president, he said:

> "From the moment the results were in and it was apparent that the African National Congress (ANC) was to form the government, I saw my mission as one of preaching reconciliation, of binding the wounds of the country, of engendering trust and confidence . . . I told the white audiences that we needed them and did not want them to leave the country. They were South Africans just like ourselves, and this was their land too . . . I said over and over that we should forget the past and concentrate on building a better future for all."

Thoughts & Discussion:

1. Perhaps you are dealing with un-forgiveness. Something happened to you, or someone did something to you that you are angry about. After learning about the story of Nelson Mandela what do you think or how do you feel now about the choice to forgive?

_____
_____
_____

2. Being a leader is about relationships. And quality relationships include the need to forgive from time to time. Perhaps this lesson reminded you about people you need to forgive? Or maybe you thought of others that you need to ask for forgiveness? Take a first step by writing their names here.

_____
_____
_____

3. Nelson Mandela said: "Resentment is like drinking poison and then hoping it will kill your enemies." What does he mean?

_____
_____
_____

SESSION TEN

"It does not take a village to raise a child, but one child can raise up a whole village."
– R.R. Ramos

Destiny and the Power of One

Purpose: This last session is about story telling. It's an opportunity to allow the power of stories to inspire us about the impact one person can make on a multitude of people.

History is full of individuals whose legacy demonstrates destiny and the power of one. It's truly amazing what one person can do when they use their imagination and follow their dreams and vision.

One of the most common and interesting traits about individuals who've made such a huge impact on the world is that they either stepped away from a place of wealth, privilege and comfort, or they were born in poverty and rose up from humble, small, and obscure beginnings.

Moses, the great prophet of the nation of Israel, was raised with wealth, the best education, and all the privileges of the son of the mighty Egyptian Pharaoh. Yet, his mark on the world was not made from that place of power and privilege, but rather from a position of poverty. His is a great story of one who stepped down from a position of wealth to step up with the poor, his own people, the slaves of Egypt, to set them free from slavery and the oppression of Pharaoh.

Mahatma Ghandi was the son of a senior government official and raised in a merchant middle-class community. He attended law school and earned a law degree in London. Yet, despite his education, he chose to live among the poor, fight for civil rights, expand the rights of women, and end discrimination against his people. He was arrested for his efforts and sent to prison. He renounced all worldly goods and wealth, organized the peasant farmers, and single handedly brought down the powerful British empire, winning his country's independence from their oppressive rule without firing a shot or conducting any violence whatsoever.

Oprah Winfrey, probably one of the most well-known women in the world, continues to achieve at the top of her industry as a TV icon as well as a successful businesswoman, entrepreneur, philanthropist, and founder of a leadership institute for young girls in Africa. Her influence in a variety of circles spans the globe:

> According to Forbes Magazine, Oprah was the richest African American of the 20th century and the world's only black billionaire for three years running. Life Magazine hailed her as the most influential woman of her generation. In 2005, Business Week named her the greatest black philanthropist in American history.

Oprah Winfrey is one person touching thousands upon tens of thousands of lives. Yet, she did not begin at the top. She was born in poverty, lived in obscurity, suffered and overcame childhood sexual abuse to eventually make her mark in the world as a leader among leaders.

Mother Teresa was probably the most respected and loved woman in the world. Her life was dedicated to living among and serving the "poorest of the poor." She founded the Missionaries of Charity. In 2012 her organization consisted of over 4,500 sisters serving in 133 countries providing care for people with HIV/AIDS, leprosy, and tuberculosis. Mother Teresa followed what she once described as a "call within the call" she received while she was traveling on a train. In her first years of leadership, she had no money and often had to beg for resources. She endured these and many more years of trials to be recognized around the world as a force for good to those suffering the pain and agony of disease. Thus, once again, we see how destiny and *the power of one* can impact the many from a position of poverty.

Cesar Estrada Chavez the Latino hero credited with moving a whole nation as he led the first successful farm workers union in U.S. history.

Cesar was also born in poverty on a small farm near Yuma, Arizona. At the age of ten, Cesar began working with his parents as a farm worker during the great depression. Cesar left school after the eighth grade to help support his family.

Cesar was laboring in apricot orchards outside San Jose, California, when he met Fred Ross, an organizer for the Community Service Organization (CSO), a barrio-based, self-help group. Within several months, Cesar was a full-time organizer with CSO and served as CSO national director in the late 1950s and early 1960s.

However, he never forgot where he had come from and his real dream to create an organization to help farm workers whose scars of suffering, he shared. In 1962, he resigned as CSO national director. He moved his wife and eight young children to Delano, California where he founded the United Farm Workers Union (UFW).

As leader of the UFW, Cesar traveled throughout California to organize farm workers, conduct rallies, and strike boycotts against the unjust conditions of farm workers. By 1975, millions of American adults joined his call for boycotts. By the early 1980s, farm workers numbered in the tens of thousands working under UFW contracts with higher pay, family health coverage, pension benefits, and other contract protections.

In October 2012, President Obama memorialized the great work of Cesar when he announced the Cesar E. Chavez National Monument at La Paz in Keene, California—the union's headquarters in Kern County's Tehachapi Mountains, east of the city of Bakersfield.

These are but a few examples of this peculiar connection between destiny, poverty, and *the power of one* individual following their purpose and dreams, and using their vision, and imagination to serve the poor. There's something special about it. There's something powerful about individuals who embrace the poor that seems to produce a quality of greatness in them that the rich don't possess.

Why do you need to know this?
Because although as a minority we've been marginalized from the mainstreams of society, never think that it means we've been marginalized from true power and the ability to achieve great things.

Being a minority is not being inferior in any way as a person. As a matter of fact, the poor and oppressed have been given their own "privileged" positioned to receive what are called "the true riches" of life.

In other words:
- Minorities _____ the community cry in a way the wealthy don't.
- They _____ the community needs in a way the privileged can't.
- They _____ the solution from a perspective in which the rich are blinded.

The Need for More and Better Leadership
This capacity, this gift of empathy we possess for the hurting, is not to be taken lightly. We should never underestimate what powerful things can happen when just one person sees a problem and has the heart and spirit to get up and do something about it.

What we have experienced from the political leaders in the highest offices of our generation of turmoil, natural disasters, wars, and financial collapse, is failure and favoritism for the privileged few and not the needy majority. That's not leadership but rather abandonment of the principles that made America great.

So now it's your turn:
- The un_____
- The un_____
- The un_____
- The under_____
- The under_____

We understand and have lived with the challenges of the poor and oppressed. And now as new leaders we have an opportunity to restore the principles of equality, liberty and justice for all, and by these principles to restore the health of the nation.

In poverty:
- We lost childhood friends that never had a chance to _____ themselves into a bigger and better lifestyle.
- Many migrant families come here seeking a better life but never seem to escape the struggles and _____ blocks of assimilation, discrimination, and marginalization.

The pathway out of poverty
- As new _____ we can continue the process of _____ and _____ other young leaders who will reach out and continue to _____ other leaders.
- The pathway is a _____ process, but an effective one if we don't quit.

The Process of Replanting Trees
For every tree that is cut or burned down, a new tree is planted to replace it. Yes, it will take years before that tree grows to replace the one removed, but grow it will, and in this way, we at least assure ourselves the hope of new beginnings, new life, and new possibilities.

Community Leaders Give Back and Put Back
By developing more leaders, we replace the lives of all those we've lost to the evil jaws of poverty and violence and to restore hope for families in desperate need of solutions.

Our Message to the Forces of Discrimination:
No matter the discrimination we face, we will continue to farm our communities, plowing the minds, cultivating the hearts, planting new seeds, watering them, growing them, and harvesting a new crop of young men and women leaders' season after season.

How and where do I get started?
There are any number of ways you can give back in creating opportunities to help lead others from the *margins to the mainstream* of American life for many youths and families.

Practical Suggestions to Give Back to Your Community

- Help create a nonprofit organization to address a need the community is concerned with, or support one already in existence by donating time as a volunteer, board member and/or financially give to the organization.
- Organize your church to do outreach for at-risk youth or create a ministry to provide needed services for neighborhood youth.
- Develop a foundation to award scholarships and grants to sustain the work of individuals and organizations committed to at-risk youth and families or support one already in existence.
- Use your talents to give presentations at schools to inspire and motivate youth to higher levels of thinking, dreaming, and goal setting.
- Volunteer to monitor, supervise, and interact with youth at school campuses before, during, or after school.
- Become a mentor to one fatherless, motherless, troubled youth.
- Support a local youth sports team or create a brand-new youth league.

My Story: Destiny and the Power of One
Finally, destiny and the power of one can be a little difficult to understand and explain, but it's amazing how it works in our lives. It ties people's lives together in unknown and mysterious ways.

Indulge me for one more story about this…my story…

Below is an article from a Los Angeles newspaper in 1956…

"POLICE RACE TRAIN, SAVE TOT ON TRACKS"

Two policemen who paused for a few minutes on their way to a shooting call were credited today with saving the life of 2-year-old Richard Ramos. Officers Fernando Najera and Robert Vernon were roaring along Marmion Way on their way to the reported shooting when they saw the youngster strolling along the Santa Fe tracks that parallel the street. Bearing down on the boy was a freight train. Vernon outraced the train and when he slammed on the brakes, Najera piled out, scrambled down the embankment, and knocked the child clear of the train as it passed. The youngster had become frozen in terror when he heard the train's whistle. The officers turned the wailing youngster over to neighbors who took him to his parents, Mr. and Mrs. Antonio Ramos of 4579 N. Figueroa Street.

The irony of my story is the fact that my salvation that day was tied to the tragedy of someone else getting shot. The newspaper story above said, *"Officers Fernando Najera and Robert Vernon were roaring along . . . on their way to a reported shooting when they saw the youngster strolling along the Santa Fe tracks . . ."*

Obviously, I don't know anything about who was shot that day, or if someone was killed (I pray not), but if that shooting had not taken place when and where it did, those two officers would not have been "roaring along" and quite possibly would not have out raced the train and gotten to me on time.

My life was saved that day by this incredible string of events. My story helps me understand that I should never take my life for granted nor should I take lightly the opportunity to go out of my way to help others. In stopping to help another, I just never know whose life I might save or change and the greatness that might be unlocked in their life to the benefit of others.

But the story doesn't end there…fast forward ten years…

A friend of mine had received a new BB gun for his birthday. For no reason at all, we decided to try it out by shooting and breaking the windows of some newly built apartments in our neighborhood. We were hiding behind a wall as we took turns shooting at the windows—when, suddenly to our shocking surprise—a cop jumped over the wall!

"What do you think you guys are doing!!" he yelled. We both stood there frozen and red-faced. "What's your name?" he asked me. "Richard", I said trembling.

"Richard what?" "Richard Ramos", I said. The expression suddenly changed on his angry face. "You're Richard Ramos?" "What's your mother's name", he asked.

"Mary", I said. That was all he needed to know…guess who it was? Yup. The same cop who had saved my life on the train tracks all those years ago!

You see, that's how the *mystery of destiny and the power of one* works. It's truly amazing how one person can affect the life of another who goes on to save and effect the life of others and on and on it goes.

Now, here we are, together, finding each other through these lessons. Coincidence? I don't think so.

Consider this:
- We are only individuals, but somehow, we are all _____ with a purpose and _____ that goes beyond our individuality.
- I am me; you are you, and we are _____. Unless we live in that understanding, we can miss living in our true-life _____.

Therefore, you can't waste time with all the distractions and negative lifestyles out there that are pulling you into their web of destruction. You're not here for that. You weren't born for that. You weren't made for that. Yet, evil does exist, and it's not on your side. It has destroyed many others, and it will destroy you too if you let it.

Our Destiny
But that's why you're reading my story. Because my life was saved to show up and interfere with and interrupt the same evil that tried to destroy my life all those years ago:
- Our lives were meant to _____.
- Our lives were meant to _____.
- Through our connection, many others will _____.

Like so many others before you I've met and connected with, it's your time to change, grow, turn, and be free to soar to the heights of the life in which you were destined.

When those hard times of life come remember:
- You are not on this earth by _____.

- You were born on purpose, with a _____.
- Our life destiny was meant for each other and many _____.

Therefore, you must go on, you must continue, you must overcome because someone else out there is depending on your life to touch and improve theirs, and around and around goes the circle of life. They don't know it yet, you don't know them yet, but somehow your life makes the difference in theirs.

Time to Answer the Call
Your destiny has arrived. Your call has come. The future is now. The future is you. It's never too late!

Never underestimate your power as an individual to have great influence on the many. All your life you've been taught that 1 + 1 = 2. However, I'm here to tell that 1 + 1 always has the potential to explode far beyond just 2!

Maybe that's beyond your understanding right now, but that's the nice part about destiny and the power of one. You don't have to understand it all for it to work its magic in you. You owe it to yourself to discover the real you, develop yourself, dream big, and walk in your destiny. So now, you're ready…go, run, fly, and lead!

About Richard R. Ramos

Overcoming the obstacles of barrio youth gangs, drugs and violence, Richard R. Ramos has devoted his career to serving high-risk youth & families. He is recognized as a national and international expert on preventing youth violence. He is the author of *From the Margins to the Mainstream – Preparing Latino Youth for Leadership in The Twenty-First Century*, as well as two books on gang prevention and intervention

In July 2003 Ramos Founded the Latino Coalition for Community Leadership, a national intermediary nonprofit. Over his twenty-year tenure the LCCL granted over $105 million dollars in grants to over 220 grassroots nonprofits in numerous cities throughout the United States.

He is the author of, *Parents on a Mission – How Parents Can Win the Competition for the Heart, Mind, and Loyalty of Their Children*, and founder of "Parents on a Mission" (POM), and "Youth on a Mission", Train the Trainer leadership programs developing parent and youth mentors. POM has been adopted by school districts, nonprofits, the Pennsylvania and Colorado Department of Corrections, Kern County Sheriff Department, and most recently by the United States Agency for International Development (USAID) in Guatemala, and Bureau of International Narcotics and Law Enforcement, U.S. Department of State in El Salvador.

Ramos has served as a Correctional Officer in California State and Federal prisons, Juvenile Hall instructor, at-risk school counselor; a co-founding director of a gang intervention/prevention community coalition; Director of a Latino youth and family teen center, and a founding director of the Interfaith Initiative of Santa Barbara County. For his decades of community service and his work in the field of human rights, he has received numerous accolades and awards including recognition by the White House Administration, The United States Congress, The California State Assembly, the Santa Barbara Hispanic Chamber of Commerce, and has been inducted into the Morehouse College's Martin Luther King, Jr. International Chapels Board.

For more information & resources visit: www.richardrramos.com
Or contact via email: richard@richardrramos.com

www.ingramcontent.com/pod-product-compliance
Lightning Source LLC
Chambersburg PA
CBHW060530010526
44110CB00052B/2553